Private Music Teacher's Yearly Bookkeeping Book

Created By Eric Michael Roberts

Published by Studio 43, LLC
www.studio43.org

ISBN-13:
978-1484933923

ISBN-10:
1484933923

Contents

Introduction

If you do not keep track of the payments, you risk loosing money! Keeping track of payments and yearly expenses is very important if you want to run a successful business. Also, when you closely track expenses, you will have more tax benefits.

I used this method for many years while teaching thousands of lessons and it works great! It will help you track payments so that you do not loose track of the money owed to you and you will be able to quickly prepare your taxes each year.

If you would like special tips to grow your student base and market your music lesson business, please read my book titled "21 Tips to Start, Build and Market Your Music Lesson Business" available on Kindle and Amazon.com and from www.21bookseries.com

How to Use Lesson Tracking Sheet

Not only will you use this sheet to track your payments and attendance, you will use it to track your schedule. You can keep all of your information in one place. I have developed special shorthand symbols to help you keep track of all your important information.

In the beginning of the month, fill out the dates of the month under the WK1 heading and put your schedule in the time column. Put your open spots on the list too (example 5:00 open). You will try to fill this spot! If a student quits mid-month and a new student signs up for the spot, simply put that new student in the lower lines as shown with the new student Jack White.

I use the special notation "OUT" when a student misses a lesson but let me know in advance that they will be missing their lesson.

I use the special notation "NS" for a now show! This is self-explanatory.

I use the "No Lesson" slash when a student was not going to take a lesson or it is a week when they were not enrolled for lessons.

I often mark the method of payment that I receive. I write "cash" or the check number in the payment column.

I like to write the amount they pay in the lesson block of the day they pay. This allows me to keep track of the exact day that a student has paid. If you are giving lesson by the week or a just a few lessons in the month, this makes it easier to count the lessons and match it with when they own next. When doing a pay-as-you-go lesson scenario (which I do not advise) or a student gets off of the regular payment schedule you can place a dollar sign ($) in the lesson block to remind you when their next payment is due. I also write in the amount in the Total column.

Examples:

I have completed an example month for February Tuesdays on the next page. I will explain some of my markings here.

Brad paid in the beginning of the month but only attended 2 lessons. He was a NO SHOW for the last two lessons of the month. In this case, I would call him to see if he was returning the next month. If not, I can open this spot for a new student.

Example Daily Record

Month _February 2013_ Day _____ Tuesdays _____

Time	Student	WK1 7	WK2 14	WK3 21	WK4 28	WK5 ✗	Total
3:30	John Smith	✔	₿80	✔	✔		₿80
4:00	Todd Merrit	₿80	✔	✔	✔		Cash ₿80
4:30	Anna Berry	₿80	✔	✔	out		₿80
5:00	open						
5:30	Emily Fredericks	╲	╲	₿120	✔		#2356 ₿120+
6:00	Brad Pendent	₿80	✔	NS	NS		₿80
4:30	NEW—Jack White	╲	╲	╲	₿20		cash ₿20

NS = No Show

✔ = Completed Lesson

 = No Lesson

Total Income ₿460

Student Information

Name	Phone
Address	
Email	
Name	Phone
Address	
Email	
Name	Phone
Address	
Email	
Name	Phone
Address	
Email	
Name	Phone
Address	
Email	
Name	Phone
Address	
Email	
Name	Phone
Address	
Email	
Name	Phone
Address	
Email	
Name	Phone
Address	
Email	
Name	Phone
Address	
Email	

Student Information

Name	Phone
Address	
Email	
Name	Phone
Address	
Email	
Name	Phone
Address	
Email	
Name	Phone
Address	
Email	
Name	Phone
Address	
Email	
Name	Phone
Address	
Email	
Name	Phone
Address	
Email	
Name	Phone
Address	
Email	
Name	Phone
Address	
Email	
Name	Phone
Address	
Email	

Student Information

Name	Phone
Address	
Email	
Name	Phone
Address	
Email	
Name	Phone
Address	
Email	
Name	Phone
Address	
Email	
Name	Phone
Address	
Email	
Name	Phone
Address	
Email	
Name	Phone
Address	
Email	
Name	Phone
Address	
Email	
Name	Phone
Address	
Email	
Name	Phone
Address	
Email	

Student Information

Name	Phone
Address	
Email	

Name	Phone
Address	
Email	

Name	Phone
Address	
Email	

Name	Phone
Address	
Email	

Name	Phone
Address	
Email	

Name	Phone
Address	
Email	

Name	Phone
Address	
Email	

Name	Phone
Address	
Email	

Name	Phone
Address	
Email	

Name	Phone
Address	
Email	

Student Information

Name	Phone
Address	
Email	
Name	Phone
Address	
Email	
Name	Phone
Address	
Email	
Name	Phone
Address	
Email	
Name	Phone
Address	
Email	
Name	Phone
Address	
Email	
Name	Phone
Address	
Email	
Name	Phone
Address	
Email	
Name	Phone
Address	
Email	
Name	Phone
Address	
Email	

Student Information

Name	Phone
Address	
Email	
Name	Phone
Address	
Email	
Name	Phone
Address	
Email	
Name	Phone
Address	
Email	
Name	Phone
Address	
Email	
Name	Phone
Address	
Email	
Name	Phone
Address	
Email	
Name	Phone
Address	
Email	
Name	Phone
Address	
Email	
Name	Phone
Address	
Email	

Student Information

Name	Phone
Address	
Email	

Name	Phone
Address	
Email	

Name	Phone
Address	
Email	

Name	Phone
Address	
Email	

Name	Phone
Address	
Email	

Name	Phone
Address	
Email	

Name	Phone
Address	
Email	

Name	Phone
Address	
Email	

Name	Phone
Address	
Email	

Name	Phone
Address	
Email	

Month_____

Year _____

Month_____ Day _____

Time	Student	WK1	WK2	WK3	WK4	WK5	Total

NS = No Show

 = Completed Lesson

◻ = No Lesson

Total Income

Month_____ Day _____

Time	Student	WK1	WK2	WK3	WK4	WK5	Total

NS = No Show

 = Completed Lesson

 = No Lesson

Total Income

Month_____ Day _____

Time	Student	WK1	WK2	WK3	WK4	WK5	Total

NS = No Show

✔ = Completed Lesson

 = No Lesson

Total Income

Month_____ Day _____

Time	Student	WK1	WK2	WK3	WK4	WK5	Total

NS = No Show

 = Completed Lesson

= No Lesson

Total Income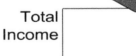

Month_____ Day _____

Time	Student	WK1	WK2	WK3	WK4	WK5	Total

NS = No Show

 = Completed Lesson

 = No Lesson

Total Income

Month_____ Day _____

Time	Student	WK1	WK2	WK3	WK4	WK5	Total

NS = No Show

 = Completed Lesson

☑ = No Lesson

Total Income

End of Month Report

Month_____ Year _____

Misc. Monthly Expense Record

Date	Note	Amt.

Total Monthly Expenses _____

Gross Monthly Income _____

Net Monthly Profit _____

Notes:

Notes:

Month_____

Year _____

Month_____ Day _____

Time	Student	WK1	WK2	WK3	WK4	WK5	Total

NS = No Show

 = Completed Lesson

 = No Lesson

Total Income

Month_____ Day _____

Time	Student	WK1	WK2	WK3	WK4	WK5	Total

NS = No Show

 = Completed Lesson

◪ = No Lesson

Total Income

Month_____ Day _____

Time	Student	WK1	WK2	WK3	WK4	WK5	Total

NS = No Show

 = Completed Lesson

= No Lesson

Total Income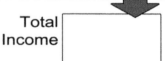

Month_____ Day _____

Time	Student	WK1	WK2	WK3	WK4	WK5	Total

NS = No Show

 = Completed Lesson

= No Lesson

Total Income

Month_____ Day _____

Time	Student	WK1	WK2	WK3	WK4	WK5	Total

NS = No Show

 = Completed Lesson

▨ = No Lesson

Total Income

Month_____ Day _____

Time	Student	WK1	WK2	WK3	WK4	WK5	Total

NS = No Show

 = Completed Lesson

 = No Lesson

Total Income

End of Month Report

Month_____ Year _____

Misc. Monthly Expense Record

Date	Note	Amt.

Total Monthly Expenses   _____

Gross Monthly Income   _____

Net Monthly Profit   _____

Notes:

Notes:

Month_____

Year _____

Month_____ Day _____

Time	Student	WK1	WK2	WK3	WK4	WK5	Total

NS = No Show

 = Completed Lesson

Total
Income

☐ = No Lesson

Month_____ Day _____

Time	Student	WK1	WK2	WK3	WK4	WK5	Total

NS = No Show

 = Completed Lesson

 = No Lesson

Total Income

Month_____ Day _____

Time	Student	WK1	WK2	WK3	WK4	WK5	Total

NS = No Show

 = Completed Lesson

◹ = No Lesson

Total Income

Month_____ Day _____

Time	Student	WK1	WK2	WK3	WK4	WK5	Total

NS = No Show

 = Completed Lesson

◻ = No Lesson

Total Income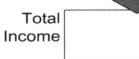

Month_____ Day _____

Time	Student	WK1	WK2	WK3	WK4	WK5	Total

NS = No Show

 = Completed Lesson

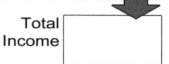

☐ = No Lesson

Total Income

Month_____ Day _____

Time	Student	WK1	WK2	WK3	WK4	WK5	Total

NS = No Show

 = Completed Lesson

 = No Lesson

Total Income

End of Month Report

Month_____ Year _____

Misc. Monthly Expense Record

Date	Note	Amt.

Total Monthly Expenses _____

Gross Monthly Income _____

Net Monthly Profit _____

Notes:

Notes:

Month_____

Year _____

Month_____ Day _____

Time	Student	WK1	WK2	WK3	WK4	WK5	Total

NS = No Show

 = Completed Lesson

= No Lesson

Total Income

Month_____ Day _____

Time	Student	WK1	WK2	WK3	WK4	WK5	Total

NS = No Show

 = Completed Lesson

= No Lesson

Total Income

Month_____ Day _____

Time	Student	WK1	WK2	WK3	WK4	WK5	Total

NS = No Show

  = Completed Lesson

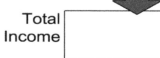

☐ = No Lesson

Total Income

Month_____ Day _____

Time	Student	WK1	WK2	WK3	WK4	WK5	Total

NS = No Show

 = Completed Lesson

 = No Lesson

Total Income

Month_____ Day _____

Time	Student	WK1	WK2	WK3	WK4	WK5	Total

NS = No Show

 = Completed Lesson

 = No Lesson

Total Income

Month_____ Day _____

Time	Student	WK1	WK2	WK3	WK4	WK5	Total

NS = No Show

 = Completed Lesson

= No Lesson

Total Income

End of Month Report

Month_____ Year _____

Misc. Monthly Expense Record

Date	Note	Amt.

Total Monthly Expenses _____

Gross Monthly Income _____

Net Monthly Profit _____

Notes:

Notes:

Month_____

Year _____

Month_____ Day _____

Time	Student	WK1	WK2	WK3	WK4	WK5	Total

NS = No Show

 = Completed Lesson

 = No Lesson

Total Income

Month_____ Day _____

Time	Student	WK1	WK2	WK3	WK4	WK5	Total

NS = No Show

✔ = Completed Lesson

 = No Lesson

Total Income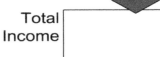

Month_____ Day _____

Time	Student	WK1	WK2	WK3	WK4	WK5	Total

NS = No Show

 = Completed Lesson

= No Lesson

Total
Income

Month_____ Day _____

Time	Student	WK1	WK2	WK3	WK4	WK5	Total

NS = No Show

 = Completed Lesson

 = No Lesson

Total Income

Month_____ Day _____

Time	Student	WK1	WK2	WK3	WK4	WK5	Total

NS = No Show

 = Completed Lesson

= No Lesson

Total Income

Month_____ Day _____

Time	Student	WK1	WK2	WK3	WK4	WK5	Total

NS = No Show

 = Completed Lesson

= No Lesson

Total Income

End of Month Report

Month_____ Year _____

Misc. Monthly Expense Record

Date	Note	Amt.

Total Monthly Expenses _____

Gross Monthly Income _____

Net Monthly Profit _____

Notes:

_____
_____
_____
_____
_____
_____
_____
_____
_____
_____
_____
_____
_____
_____
_____
_____
_____
_____

Notes:

Month_____

Year _____

Month_____ Day _____

Time	Student	WK1	WK2	WK3	WK4	WK5	Total

NS = No Show

 = Completed Lesson

= No Lesson

Total Income

Month_____ Day _____

Time	Student	WK1	WK2	WK3	WK4	WK5	Total

NS = No Show

 = Completed Lesson

 = No Lesson

Total Income

Month_____ Day _____

Time	Student	WK1	WK2	WK3	WK4	WK5	Total

NS = No Show

 = Completed Lesson

◻ = No Lesson

Total Income

Month_____ Day _____

Time	Student	WK1	WK2	WK3	WK4	WK5	Total

NS = No Show

 = Completed Lesson

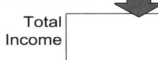

☐ = No Lesson

Total Income

Month_____ Day _____

Time	Student	WK1	WK2	WK3	WK4	WK5	Total

NS = No Show

 = Completed Lesson

= No Lesson

Total Income

Month_____ Day _____

Time	Student	WK1	WK2	WK3	WK4	WK5	Total

NS = No Show

 = Completed Lesson

 = No Lesson

Total Income

End of Month Report

Month_____ Year _____

Misc. Monthly Expense Record

Date	Note	Amt.

Total Monthly Expenses _____

Gross Monthly Income _____

Net Monthly Profit _____

Notes:

_____

_____

_____

_____

_____

_____

_____

_____

_____

_____

_____

_____

_____

_____

_____

_____

_____

_____

_____

Notes:

Month_____

Year _____

Month_____ Day _____

Time	Student	WK1	WK2	WK3	WK4	WK5	Total

NS = No Show

✔ = Completed Lesson

 = No Lesson

Total Income

Month_____ Day _____

Time	Student	WK1	WK2	WK3	WK4	WK5	Total

NS = No Show

 = Completed Lesson

 = No Lesson

Total Income

Month_____ Day _____

Time	Student	WK1	WK2	WK3	WK4	WK5	Total

NS = No Show

 = Completed Lesson

 = No Lesson

Total Income

Month_____ Day _____

Time	Student	WK1	WK2	WK3	WK4	WK5	Total

NS = No Show

 = Completed Lesson

 = No Lesson

Total Income

Month_____ Day _____

Time	Student	WK1	WK2	WK3	WK4	WK5	Total

NS = No Show

✔ = Completed Lesson

 = No Lesson

Total Income

Month_____ Day _____

Time	Student	WK1	WK2	WK3	WK4	WK5	Total

NS = No Show

 = Completed Lesson

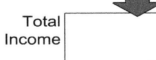

= No Lesson

Total Income

End of Month Report

Month_____ Year _____

Misc. Monthly Expense Record

Date	Note	Amt.

Total Monthly Expenses _____

Gross Monthly Income _____

Net Monthly Profit _____

Notes:

Notes:

Month_____

Year _____

Month_____ Day _____

Time	Student	WK1	WK2	WK3	WK4	WK5	Total

NS = No Show

 = Completed Lesson

☑ = No Lesson

Total Income

Month_____ Day _____

Time	Student	WK1	WK2	WK3	WK4	WK5	Total

NS = No Show

 = Completed Lesson

☐ = No Lesson

Total Income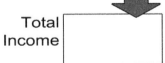

Month_____ Day _____

Time	Student	WK1	WK2	WK3	WK4	WK5	Total

NS = No Show

  = Completed Lesson

= No Lesson

Total Income

Month_____ Day _____

Time	Student	WK1	WK2	WK3	WK4	WK5	Total

NS = No Show

 = Completed Lesson

 = No Lesson

Total Income

Month_____ Day _____

Time	Student	WK1	WK2	WK3	WK4	WK5	Total

NS = No Show

 = Completed Lesson

Total Income

□ = No Lesson

Month_____ Day _____

Time	Student	WK1	WK2	WK3	WK4	WK5	Total

NS = No Show

 = Completed Lesson

= No Lesson

Total Income

End of Month Report

Month_____ Year _____

Misc. Monthly Expense Record

Date	Note	Amt.

Total Monthly Expenses _____

Gross Monthly Income _____

Net Monthly Profit _____

Notes:

_____

_____

_____

_____

_____

_____

_____

_____

_____

_____

_____

_____

_____

_____

_____

_____

_____

_____

_____

_____

Notes:

Month_____

Year _____

Month_____ Day _____

Time	Student	WK1	WK2	WK3	WK4	WK5	Total

NS = No Show

 = Completed Lesson

= No Lesson

Total Income

Month_____ Day _____

Time	Student	WK1	WK2	WK3	WK4	WK5	Total

NS = No Show

 = Completed Lesson

 = No Lesson

Total Income

Month_____ Day _____

Time	Student	WK1	WK2	WK3	WK4	WK5	Total

NS = No Show

 = Completed Lesson

 = No Lesson

Total Income

Month_____ Day _____

Time	Student	WK1	WK2	WK3	WK4	WK5	Total

NS = No Show

 = Completed Lesson

 = No Lesson

Total Income

Month_____ Day _____

Time	Student	WK1	WK2	WK3	WK4	WK5	Total

NS = No Show

✔ = Completed Lesson

 = No Lesson

Total Income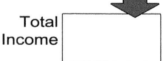

Month_____ Day _____

Time	Student	WK1	WK2	WK3	WK4	WK5	Total

NS = No Show

 = Completed Lesson

 = No Lesson

Total Income

End of Month Report

Month_____ Year _____

Misc. Monthly Expense Record

Date	Note	Amt.

Total Monthly Expenses   _____

Gross Monthly Income   _____

Net Monthly Profit   _____

Notes:

Notes:

Month_____

Year _____

Month_____ Day _____

Time	Student	WK1	WK2	WK3	WK4	WK5	Total

NS = No Show

 = Completed Lesson

 = No Lesson

Total Income

Month_____ Day _____

Time	Student	WK1	WK2	WK3	WK4	WK5	Total

NS = No Show

 = Completed Lesson

 = No Lesson

Total Income

Month_____ Day _____

Time	Student	WK1	WK2	WK3	WK4	WK5	Total

NS = No Show

 = Completed Lesson

 = No Lesson

Total Income

Month_____ Day _____

Time	Student	WK1	WK2	WK3	WK4	WK5	Total

NS = No Show

 = Completed Lesson

 = No Lesson

Total Income

Month_____ Day _____

Time	Student	WK1	WK2	WK3	WK4	WK5	Total

NS = No Show

 = Completed Lesson

◩ = No Lesson

Total Income

Month_____ Day _____

Time	Student	WK1	WK2	WK3	WK4	WK5	Total

NS = No Show

 = Completed Lesson

= No Lesson

Total Income

End of Month Report

Month_____ Year _____

Misc. Monthly Expense Record

Date	Note	Amt.

Total Monthly Expenses _____

Gross Monthly Income _____

Net Monthly Profit _____

Notes:

Notes:

Month_____

Year _____

Month_____ Day _____

Time	Student	WK1	WK2	WK3	WK4	WK5	Total

NS = No Show

 = Completed Lesson

Total Income

◻ = No Lesson

Month_____ Day _____

Time	Student	WK1	WK2	WK3	WK4	WK5	Total

NS = No Show

 = Completed Lesson

☐ = No Lesson

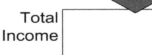

Total Income

Month_____ Day _____

Time	Student	WK1	WK2	WK3	WK4	WK5	Total

NS = No Show

 = Completed Lesson

☐ = No Lesson

Total Income

Month_____ Day _____

Time	Student	WK1	WK2	WK3	WK4	WK5	Total

NS = No Show

 = Completed Lesson

 = No Lesson

Total Income

Month_____ Day _____

Time	Student	WK1	WK2	WK3	WK4	WK5	Total

NS = No Show

 = Completed Lesson

 = No Lesson

Total Income

Month_____ Day _____

Time	Student	WK1	WK2	WK3	WK4	WK5	Total

NS = No Show

 = Completed Lesson

= No Lesson

Total Income

End of Month Report

Month_____ Year _____

Misc. Monthly Expense Record

Date	Note	Amt.

Total Monthly Expenses   _____

Gross Monthly Income   _____

Net Monthly Profit   _____

Notes:

Notes:

Month_____

Year _____

Month_____ Day _____

Time	Student	WK1	WK2	WK3	WK4	WK5	Total

NS = No Show

 = Completed Lesson

 = No Lesson

Total Income

Month_____ Day _____

Time	Student	WK1	WK2	WK3	WK4	WK5	Total

NS = No Show

✔ = Completed Lesson

 = No Lesson

Total Income

Month_____ Day _____

Time	Student	WK1	WK2	WK3	WK4	WK5	Total

NS = No Show

 = Completed Lesson

 = No Lesson

Total Income

Month_____ Day _____

Time	Student	WK1	WK2	WK3	WK4	WK5	Total

NS = No Show

 = Completed Lesson

= No Lesson

 Total Income

Month_____ Day _____

Time	Student	WK1	WK2	WK3	WK4	WK5	Total

NS   = No Show

✔   = Completed Lesson

   = No Lesson

Total Income

Month_____ Day _____

Time	Student	WK1	WK2	WK3	WK4	WK5	Total

NS = No Show

 = Completed Lesson

 = No Lesson

Total Income

End of Month Report

Month_____ Year _____

Misc. Monthly Expense Record

Date	Note	Amt.

Total Monthly Expenses _____

Gross Monthly Income _____

Net Monthly Profit _____

Notes:

Notes:

Month_____

Year _____

Month_____ Day _____

Time	Student	WK1	WK2	WK3	WK4	WK5	Total

NS = No Show

 = Completed Lesson

 = No Lesson

Total Income

Month_____ Day _____

Time	Student	WK1	WK2	WK3	WK4	WK5	Total

NS = No Show

  = Completed Lesson

  = No Lesson

Total Income

Month_____ Day _____

Time	Student	WK1	WK2	WK3	WK4	WK5	Total

NS = No Show

 = Completed Lesson

= No Lesson

Total Income

Month_____ Day _____

Time	Student	WK1	WK2	WK3	WK4	WK5	Total

NS = No Show

 = Completed Lesson

= No Lesson

Total Income

Month_____ Day _____

Time	Student	WK1	WK2	WK3	WK4	WK5	Total

NS = No Show

 = Completed Lesson

◻ = No Lesson

Total Income

Month_____ Day _____

Time	Student	WK1	WK2	WK3	WK4	WK5	Total

NS = No Show

 = Completed Lesson

◻ = No Lesson

Total Income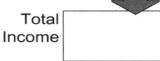

End of Month Report

Month_____ Year _____

Misc. Monthly Expense Record

Date	Note	Amt.

Total Monthly Expenses _____

Gross Monthly Income _____

Net Monthly Profit _____

Notes:

Notes:

Other Yearly Income

Date	Note	Amt.

Total Other Yearly Income _____

Other Yearly Expenses

Date	Note	Amt.

Total Other Yearly Expenses _____

Mileage Record

Date	Note	Miles
TOTAL MILES		

Total Yearly Income

Year _____

January Income	
February Income	
March Income	
April Income	
May Income	
June Income	
July Income	
August Income	
September Income	
October Income	
November Income	
December Income	
OTHER INCOME	
OTHER INCOME	
OTHER INCOME	
TOTAL INCOME	

Total Yearly Expenses

Year _____

January Expenses	
February Expenses	
March Expenses	
April Expenses	
May Expenses	
June Expenses	
July Expenses	
August Expenses	
September Expenses	
October Expenses	
November Expenses	
December Expenses	
TOTAL OTHER EXPENSES	
TOTAL EXPENSES	

END OF YEAR REPORT

YEAR _____

Total Gross Income	
Total Expenses	
TOTAL NET PROFIT	
Total Miles	

If you are teaching from your home:

Home Office Square Foot	
Home Mortgage Interest	
All Home Utilities	

Notes:

Notes:

Notes:

_____

_____

_____

_____

_____

_____

_____

_____

_____

_____

_____

_____

_____

_____

_____

_____

_____

_____

_____

_____

Notes:

Notes:

Notes:

Notes:

Notes:

Notes:

CPSIA information can be obtained
at www.ICGtesting.com
Printed in the USA
LVHW041919021218
599025LV00019B/1172/P

9 781484 933923